A LOOK AT THE BILL OF RIGHTS

The Right to PRIVACY

BY MARY GRIFFIN

CRASHCOURSE

Gareth Stevens PUBLISHING

Please visit our website, www.garethstevens.com. For a free color catalog of all our high-quality books, call toll free 1-800-542-2595 or fax 1-877-542-2596.

Library of Congress Cataloging-in-Publication Data
Names: Griffin, Mary, 1978- author.
Title: The right to privacy / Mary Griffin.
Description: Buffalo, New York : Gareth Stevens Publishing, 2026. | Series: A look at the Bill of Rights | Includes index.
Identifiers: LCCN 2024036042 | ISBN 9781482470413 (library binding) | ISBN 9781482470406 (paperback) | ISBN 9781482470420 (ebook)
Subjects: LCSH: Privacy, Right of–Juvenile literature.
Classification: LCC K3263 .G75 2026 | DDC 342.7308/58–dc23/eng/20240806
LC record available at https://lccn.loc.gov/2024036042

First Edition

Published in 2026 by
Gareth Stevens Publishing
2544 Clinton Street
Buffalo, NY 14224

Designer: Andrea Davison-Bartolotta
Editor: Kristen Rajczak Nelson

Photo credits: Cover, pp. 1, 21 (top) antoniodiaz/Shutterstock.com; series art (interior background texture) Nik Merkulov/Shutterstock.com; series art (fact box sticker) Sulovsky/Shutterstock.com; series art (blue backgrounds) Le Chernina/Shutterstock.com; series art (banners) saicle/Shutterstock.com; p. 5 Studio Romantic/Shutterstock.com; p. 7 (frame) Breyenn/Shutterstock.com; p. 7 (Madison) Prachaya Roekdeethaweesab/Shutterstock.com; p. 7 (constitution) courtesy of the National Archives; p. 9 (bottom) Cory Woodruff/Shutterstock.com; pp. 9 (top), 15 courtesy of Library of Congress; p. 11 (top) 1000 Words/Shutterstock.com; p. 11 (bottom) Joe Seer/Shutterstock.com; p. 13 Cookie Studio/Shutterstock.com; p. 17 szefei/Shutterstock.com; p. 19 (bottom) Wangkun Jia/Shutterstock.com; p. 19 (top) Everett Collection/Shutterstock.com; p. 21 (bottom) Robert Kneschke/Shutterstock.com; p. 23 Gorodenkoff/Shutterstock.com; p. 25 Erik Cox Photography/Shutterstock.com; p. 27 (bottom) Lukas Holub/Shutterstock.com; p. 27 (top) File:Supreme Court of the United States - Roberts Court 2022.jpg/Wikimedia Commons; p. 29 Jose Calsina/Shutterstock.com; p. 30 Germanroam/Shutterstock.com.

Printed in China

Some of the images in this book illustrate individuals who are models. The depictions do not imply actual situations or events.

CPSIA compliance information: Batch #QS26GS: For further information contact Gareth Stevens at 1-800-542-2595.

Contents

Words in the glossary appear in **bold** type the first time they are used in the text.

MORE THAN WHAT'S WRITTEN

Rights are the freedoms **citizens** are guaranteed, or promised, by the government. Sometimes, laws or constitutions clearly state these rights. Other times, rights are **implied**. The right to privacy is one of these rights. It's not written in any part of the U.S. Constitution!

Make the GRADE

A constitution is the basic laws by which a country or state is governed. The U.S. Constitution is the highest law in the United States.

THE CONSTITUTION

When the U.S. Constitution was written, it didn't have a list of rights guaranteed to citizens at all. Some leaders wouldn't sign the Constitution without the promise this would be added. So a member of Congress from Virginia, James Madison, wrote 17 amendments.

Make the GRADE

Amendments are changes or additions to a constitution. Twelve of Madison's 17 amendments were sent to the states to be ratified, or approved.

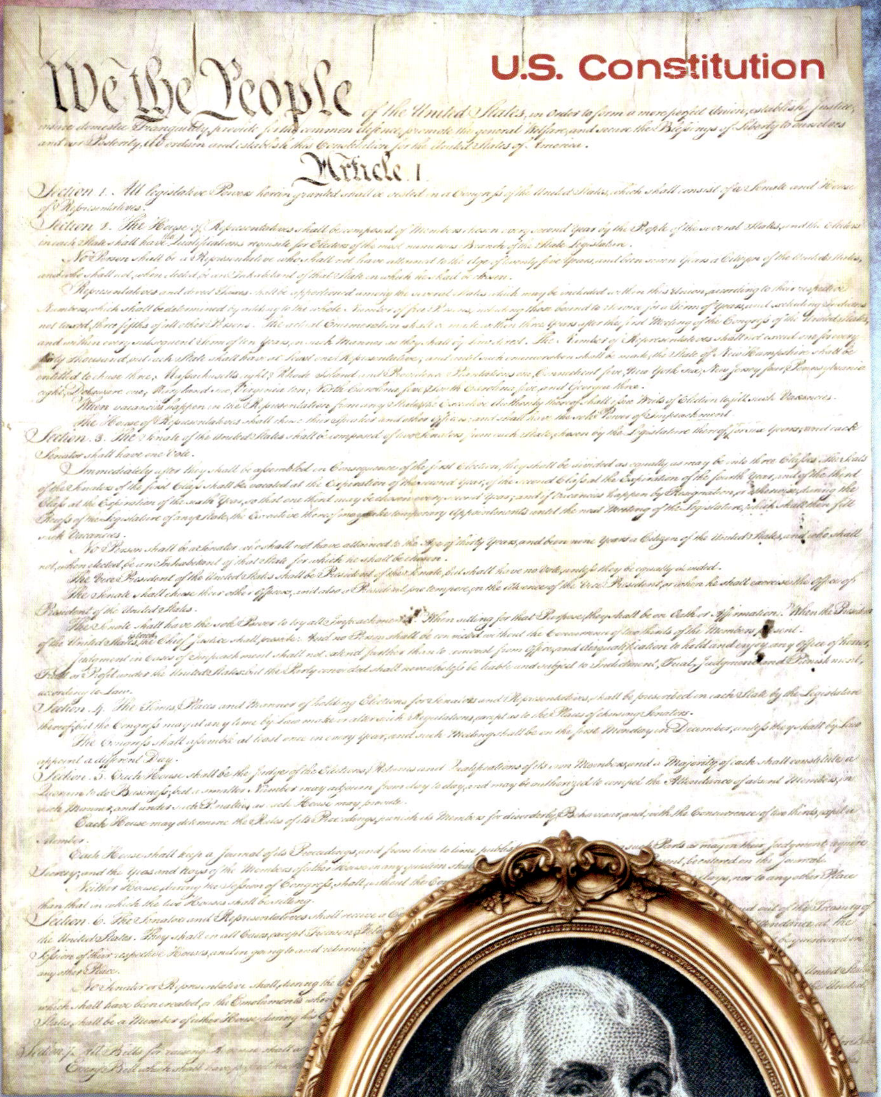

We the People of the United States, in Order to form a more perfect Union, establish Justice, insure domestic Tranquility, provide for the common defence, promote the general Welfare, and secure the Blessings of Liberty to ourselves and our Posterity, do ordain and establish this Constitution for the United States of America.

Article I

Section 1. All legislative Powers herein granted shall be vested in a Congress of the United States, which shall consist of a Senate and House of Representatives.

U.S. Constitution

James Madison

In 1791, 10 of the amendments had been ratified by enough states to become part of the Constitution. These 10 amendments became known as the Bill of Rights. It **protects** freedom of speech and the press, and granted citizens the right to **due process**, among other rights.

Make the GRADE

The United States started as British colonies. A colony is land controlled by another country.

The Bill of Rights
Amendment I
establishment of religion, or prohibiting
people peaceably to assemble, and to petition
Amendment II
the security of a free State, the right of the
Amendment III

WHAT IS PRIVACY?

In everyday use, privacy is the state of being away from people. To kids, it may mean having space that is their own. To **celebrities**, it may mean time away from the public eye. Many times, private matters are those people don't want everyone to know about.

Make the GRADE

Today privacy also means a person's ability to protect how their personal **information** is shared and used.

The "right to privacy" means something a little different. It is about the dealings between citizens and the government. It means the government doesn't unnecessarily **meddle** in citizens' lives and personal matters.

Make the GRADE

In the late 1700s, people felt the government of both Great Britain and the colonies **infringed** upon the right to privacy by searching people's belongings without a **warrant**.

Even though it's not clearly written in the Bill of Rights, James Madison and those who wrote the Constitution cared about the right to privacy. In fact, this right is part of five different amendments in the Bill of Rights!

Make the GRADE

The 14th Amendment isn't part of the Bill of Rights, but it's important to citizens' rights. It made the guarantees of the Bill of Rights apply to state governments too.

the signing of the Constitution

THE FIRST AMENDMENT

The First Amendment says Congress can't make any laws that **limit** the practice of religion, or faith. This has been **interpreted** as protecting the privacy of a citizen's beliefs. The amendment also guarantees freedom of assembly, and protects private gatherings.

Make the GRADE

The First Amendment protects freedom of speech and of the press too. These may be **extended** to protect what people read and watch in the privacy of their home.

THE THIRD AMENDMENT

The Third Amendment says in part: "No soldier shall, in time of peace be quartered in any house, without the **consent** of the owner, nor in time of war." It protects the privacy of someone's home from the government.

Make the GRADE

Quartering soldiers means being made to let soldiers stay in your home and giving them food or other things they may need.

THE FOURTH AMENDMENT

The Fourth Amendment protects citizens against unreasonable searches or taking of personal belongings. It goes on to say that searches cannot occur without a warrant or probable cause. It upholds the privacy of a person and what they own.

Make the GRADE

To have "probable cause" means to have a reasonable idea of something. For example, if a person was caught on a store camera stealing, the police may have probable cause to search that person.

POLICE

THE FIFTH AMENDMENT

In part, the Fifth Amendment says: "No person . . . shall be compelled in any criminal case to be a witness against himself." This means no one can be made to say something that will tie them to wrongdoing. It gives citizens some privacy of information.

Make the GRADE

Sometimes the government may infringe on people's rights. But it must have a very good reason for doing so, such as the safety of others.

THE NINTH AMENDMENT

The Ninth Amendment says that rights not listed in the Bill of Rights are still promised to citizens. The right to privacy is one of these rights. It's an important right the government shouldn't infringe upon.

Make the GRADE

James Madison wanted to be sure rights not clearly stated in the Bill of Rights were still protected. That's why he wrote the Ninth Amendment!

PEACE
LOVE
PRIVACY

THE HIGHEST COURT

The Supreme Court is the highest court in the United States. One of its jobs is to interpret the Constitution. The use of these amendments to protect the right to privacy has come from Supreme Court decisions. They still decide privacy cases today.

Make the GRADE

The judges who serve on the Supreme Court are called justices. They don't always agree on the outcome of a case they hear!

Supreme Court justices, 2022

Supreme Court building

YOUR PRIVACY!

If you are a U.S. citizen, you have a right to privacy, even as a young person! Sometimes you have fewer rights when you're at school. If you ever have questions about whether your rights have been infringed on, talk to an adult you trust.

Make the GRADE

Laws about privacy in school can be different from state to state.

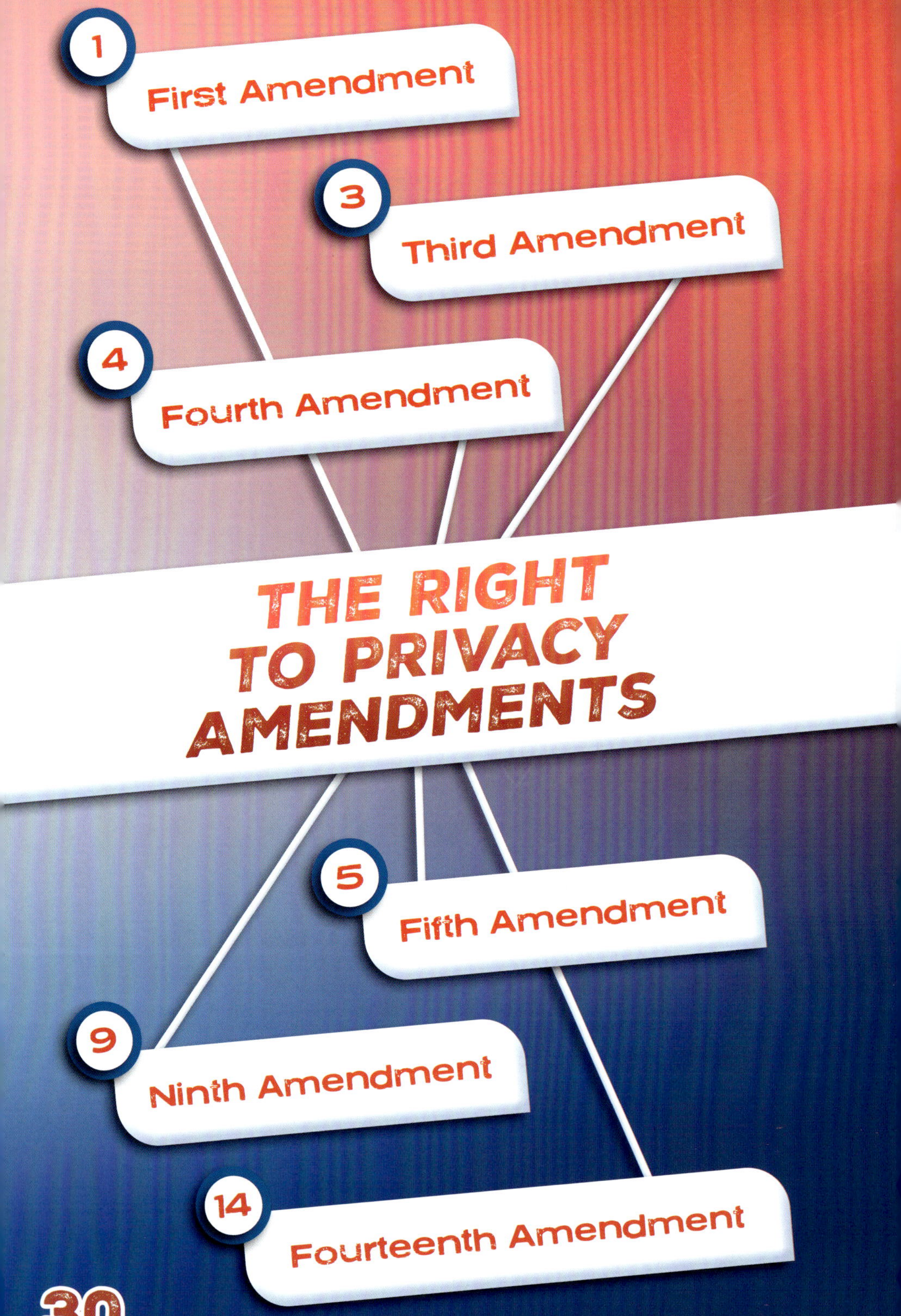
1
First Amendment
3
Third Amendment
4
Fourth Amendment
THE RIGHT TO PRIVACY AMENDMENTS
5
Fifth Amendment
9
Ninth Amendment
14
Fourteenth Amendment

Glossary

celebrity: A person who is well-known for some reason.

citizen: Someone who lives in a country legally and has certain rights.

consent: To agree to allow something.

due process: The official way of doing things within the law.

extend: To stretch out.

imply: To mean but not say clearly.

information: Knowledge obtained from study or observation.

infringe: To wrongly limit or stop.

interpret: To tell the meaning of something.

limit: To stop or keep from happening.

meddle: To get involved in when involvement is not wanted.

protect: To keep safe.

warrant: An official piece of paper from a court that allows police to do something such as a search.

For More Information

Books

Knopp, Ezra E. *The U.S. Constitution.* Buffalo, NY: Britannica Educational Publishing, 2024.

Walton, Kathryn. *The Bill of Rights.* Buffalo, NY: Enslow Publishing, 2024.

Website

Bill of Rights
https://bensguide.gpo.gov/bill-of-rights-1789-91
Check out this short guide to all the amendments included in the Bill of Rights.

Publisher's note to educators and parents: Our editors have carefully reviewed these websites to ensure that they are suitable for students. Many websites change frequently, however, and we cannot guarantee that a site's future contents will continue to meet our high standards of quality and educational value. Be advised that students should be closely supervised whenever they access the internet.

Index